March of America Facsimile Series

Number 32

Good Order Established
in Pennsilvania & New-Jersey

Thomas Budd

Good Order Established
in Pennsilvania
& New-Jersey
by Thomas Budd

ANN ARBOR

UNIVERSITY MICROFILMS, INC.

A Subsidiary of Xerox Corporation

56755

Foreword

Good Order Established in Pennsilvania & New-Jersey in America, written by Thomas Budd, was printed in 1685 by Philadelphia's first printer, William Bradford. Though Budd had several purposes in mind when he wrote the book, his primary object was to attract emigrants from England.

Budd had, himself, emigrated from England sometime prior to 1678 and settled in New Jersey, where he played a prominent role in the economic and political life of the colony. The year before publishing his book, he moved to Philadelphia. Therefore he could speak with some authority about conditions in New Jersey and Pennsylvania. He devoted a considerable part of the treatise to a description of economic opportunities. The colonies offered relief, he thought, for "the distressed Condition that many thousand families lie under in my Native Country, by reason of the deadness of Trade, and want of work." A Quaker at the time he wrote this treatise, Budd knew that many prospective emigrants would find it reassuring to learn that these two colonies had "certain fundamental Laws, by which every Man's Liberty and Property...are preserved: so that none shall be hurt in his Person, Estate, or Liberty for his Religious Persuasion or Practice in Worship towards God."

Budd minimized some of the supposed hazards of life in the New World. Settlers need not fear the Indians, he said. They "are but few in Number, and have been very serviceable to us." He was engagingly frank in pointing out certain annoyances, however. The marshes of New Jersey, he admitted, were infested by "small Flies, called Musketoes, which are troublesome to such People as are not used to them." But with his usual optimism, he suggested that the mosquito problem could be eliminated by draining and cultivating the marsh lands.

Budd understood that emigration required capital. He tried to show potential investors in England how they could realize a handsome return on their money by financing such enterprises and at the same time serve a higher purpose by bringing men "out of that Slavery and Poverty they groan under."

Full of ideas for the improvement of the colonies, Budd advocated a system of schools in which all children, even the children of the poor and the children of the Indians, could receive an education. The establishment of a bank to provide credit for accelerating the development of the region and the erection of a public storehouse in which producers and merchants could store commodities in safety were other proposals he offered.

Frederick J. Shepard has provided additional information about Budd in his edition of Thomas Budd, *Good Order Established in Pennsylvania and New Jersey* (Cleveland, 1902).

Good Order Established
in Pennsilvania & New-Jersey

Good Order Established

IN

Pennſilvania & New-Jerſey

IN

AMERICA,

Being a true Account of the Country ;
With its Produce and Commodities there made.

And the great Improvements that may be made by
means of **Publick Store-houſes** for **Hemp, Flat** and
Linnen-Cloth ; alſo, the Advantages of a **Publick-
School**, the Profits of a **Publick-Bank**, and the Probability of its ariſing, if thoſe directions here laid down are
followed. With the advantages of publick **Granaries.**

Likewiſe, ſeveral other things needful to be underſtood by
thoſe that are or do intend to be concerned in planting in
the ſaid Countries.

All which is laid down very plain, in this ſmall Treatiſe ; it
being eaſie to be underſtood by any ordinary Capacity. To
which the *Reader* is referred for his further ſatisfaction.

By Thomas Budd.

Printed in the Year **1685.**

Those that have generous Spirits, whose desires and Endeavours are to bring the Creation into Order, do I dedicate This, the first Fruits of my Endeavours.

I Taking into consideration the distressed Condition that many thousand Families lie under in my Native Country, by reason of the deadness of Trade, and want of work, and believing that many that have great store of Money that lies by them unimploy'd, would be willing and ready to assist and encourage those poor distressed People, by supplying them with Monies, in order to bring them out of that Slavery and Poverty they groan under, if they might do it with safety to themselves. These Considerations put me on writing this small Treatise, wherein I hope the Reader will have full Satisfaction, that the Rich may help to relieve the Poor, and yet reap great Profit and Advantage to themselves by their so doing, which if it so happen that Rich and Poor are benefitted by following the Advice here given, then will be answered the hearty Desires of

Your True and Well-wishing Friend,
THOMAS BUDD.

It is to be noted, that the Government of these Countries is so settled by Concessions, and such care taken by the establishment of certain fundamental Laws, by which every Man's Liberty and Property, both as Men and Christians, are preserved; so that none shall be hurt in his Person, Estate or Liberty for his Religious Perswasion or Practice in Worship towards God.

PEnnſylvania and *New-Jerſy* in *America* lieth in about forty & forty two Degrees of North Latitude, and is ſevered the one from the other by the River of *Delaware* on the Weſt, and ſeperated from *New-York* Collony by *Sandy-hoock-Bay*, and part of *Hudſons* River on the Eaſt. The dayes in the Winter are about two hours longer, and in the Summer two hours ſhorter than in *England*, the Summer ſomewhat hotter, which cauſeth the Fruits and Corn ſomewhat to ripen faſter than in *England*, and the Harveſt for *Wheat*, *Rye* and *Barley*, being about the latter end of *June*. In the Winter ſeaſon it is cold and freezing Weather, and ſometimes Snow, but commonly very clear and Sun-ſhine, which ſoon diſſolves it.

The Country is well Watered; the River of *Delaware* being navigable for Ships of great burthen to *Burlington*, which from the *Capes*, or entrance, is accounted an hundred and forty Miles ; and for Sloops to the Falls, which is about ten Miles farther.

The Bay of *Sandy-hoock* on *Eaſt-Jerſy* is a ſafe and excellent Harbour for any Fleet of Ships, which can lie there in all Weathers, and go in and out to Sea in Winter, as well as Summer, and Ships of great Burthen can lie cloſe to the Town of *New-Perth*, which renders it a good Scituation for Navigation, from whence in ſix Hours time at moſt, Ships can go out into the Sea ; and cloſe by the Town of *Perth* runs up *Rariton* River. From the Falls of *Delaware* River the *Indians* go in Cannows up the ſaid River, to an *Indian* Town called *Miniſincks*, which is accounted from the Falls about eighty Miles ; but this they perform by great Labour in ſetting up againſt the Stream ; but they can come down

with

with eafe and fpeed ; the River from the Falls runs from the North and North-Weft about twenty Miles, as I my felf obferved in my Travel fo far by the River, but by the *Indians* Information, it cometh about more Eafterly farther up. I have been informed, that about *Minifincks*, by the River-fide, both in *New-Jer/ey* and *Pennfylvania* is great quantities of exceeding rich open Land, which is occafioned by wafhing down of the Leaves and Soil in great Rains from the Mountains, which Land is exceeding good, for the raifing of *Hemp* and *Flax, Wheat,* or any other forts of Corn, Fruits, Roots *&c.* Where in time may be conveniently fettled a Manufacture for the making of *Linnen-Cloth, Cordage, Twine, Sacking, Fifhing-Nets,* and all other Commodities commonly made of Hemp or Flax : And after great Rains, we may bring down great quantities of Goods in flat-bottom-Boats, built for that purpofe, which will then come down, by reafon of the Land-floods with fpeed.

And into this River, betwixt the Capes and the Falls, run many navigable Rivers and Cricks, fome of them fifteen or twenty Miles, and others lefs, which Rivers and Cricks are made by the plenty of Springs and Brooks, that run out of the Country, many of which Brooks are fo confiderable, as to be fit to drive Mills. And above the falls, in travelling of twenty Miles by the Rivers fide, I went over twenty runnings of Water, five or fix of them being fit to build Mills on.

The Country for the moft part is pretty leavel, until we come about ten Miles above the Falls, where it is Mountanious for many Miles, but interlaced with fertile Valleys. The Bay and River of *Delaware,* and the Rivers and Cricks that runs into it, are plentifully ftored with various forts of good *Fifh* and *Water-Fowl,* as *Swans, Geefe, Ducks, Wigeons,* &c. And a confiderable *Whale*-Fifhery may be carried on in

the

the Bay of *Delaware*, and on the Sea-Coasts of *New Jersey*, there being *Whale-Fisheries* already begun, plenty of *Whales* being by experience found there, and the Winter-time being the time for the catching them, they will not thereby be hindred of raising there Summer-Crops; and the Oyl and Bone being good Commodities to be sent for *England*, there also being in the Bay of *Delaware* and *Sandy-hoock*, *Drums*, *Sheeps-heads* *Bass*, and other sorts of large Fish, which may be fit to salt up in Casks to keep for use, and Transportation also. There are great plenty of *Oysters*, which may be pickled and put up in small Casks for use. Likewise, in *Delaware* River are great plenty of *Sturgion*, which doubtless might be a good Trade, if mannaged by such Persons as are skilful in the boyling and pickling of them, so as to preserve them good to *Barbadoes*, and other adjacent Islands. There are also in the Spring great quantities of a sort of Fish like *Hexrings*; with plenty of the Fish called *Shads*, but not like the *Shads* in *England*, but of another kind, being a much better sort of Fish; the Inhabitants usually catch quantities, which they salt up, and pack them in Barrels for Winter's Provision.

The Lands from the Capes, to about six Miles above *New-Castle* (which is by estimation ninety Miles) is for the most part very rich, there being very many navigable Cricks on both sides of the River, and on the River and Cricks are great quantities of rich fat Marsh Land, which causeth those parts, to some fresh People, to be somewhat unhealthful in the latter part of the Summer, at which time some of them have *Agues*: Also in and near these Marshes, are small Flies, called *Musketoes*, which are troublesome to such People as are not used to them; but were those Marshes banked, and drained, and then plowed and sowed, some Years with Corn, and then with *English* Hay-seed, I do suppose it would

would be healthful, and very little troubled with *Musketoes*: and if Cattel did commonly feed on this Ground, and tread it as in *England*, I suppose it would not be inferior to the rich Meadows on the River of *Thames*; and were quantities of this Land laid dry, and brought into Tillage, I suppose it would bear great Crops of *Wheat*, *Pease* and *Barley*, *Hemp* and *Flax*, and it would be very fit for *Hop-Gardens*, and for *English* Grass, which might serve for rich Pastures or Meadow. Also these Marshes are fit for *Rape*, and were *Rape*-Mills built, and the design mannaged, so as it would be if it were in *England* or *Holland*, a great Trade might be carried on, and many hundred Tuns of *Rape*-Oyl might be made Yearly, and sent to *England*, to the Planters inrichment; and not only so, but would be for Merchants advantage, they thereby having Goods to freight their Ships, which would tend to the benefit of the Inhabitants in general.

And if those Trades and Designs are carried on to effect, as are mentioned in this Treatise, there would naturally follow Trade and Imployment for *Ship-wrights*, *Boat-wrights*, *Coopers*, *Carpenters*, *Smiths*, *Ropers*, *Mariners*, *Weavers*, *Butchers*, *Bakers*, *Brewers*; and many other sorts of Trades would have full Imployment.

From six Miles above *New-Castle* to the Falls of *Delaware* (which is about sixty Miles) and so to the Head of the said River, the *Water* is clear, fresh, and fit for Brewing, or any other use.

The *Air* clear and good, it being supposed to be as healthful as any part of *England*.

The *Land* is in Veins, some good, and some bad, but the greatest part will bear good Corn, as *Wheat*, *Rye*, *Barley*, *Oats*, *Indian Corn*, *Buck-Wheat*, *Pease* and *Indian Beans*, &c.

Fruits that grow natural in the Countries are *Strawberries*, *Cranberries*, *Huckleberries*, *Blackberries*, *Medlers*, *Grapes*, *Plums*,

Plums, Hickery-Nuts, Walnuts, Mulberies, Cheſtnuts, Haſſel-nuts, &c.

Garden Fruits groweth well, as *Cabbage*, *Colworts*, *Colli-flowers*, *Sparagraſs*, *Carrots*, *Parſneps*, *Turnups*, *Oynions*, *Cow-cumbers*, *Pumkins*, *Water-Mellons*, *Musk-Mellons*, *Squaſhes*, *Potatoes*, *Currants*, *Gooſberries*, *Roſes*, *Cornations*, *Tulips*, Garden-Herbs, Flowers, Seeds, Fruits, &c. for ſuch as grow in *England*, certainly will grow here.

Orchards of *Apples*, *Pears*, *Quinces*, *Peaches*, *Aprecocks*, *Plums*, *Cheries*, and other ſorts of the uſual Fruits of *England* may be ſoon raiſed to good advantage, the Trees growing faſter then in *England*, whereof great quantities of *Sider* may be made. And were Glaſs-houſes erected to furniſh us with Bottles, we might have a profitable Trade, by ſending *Sider* to *Jamaico* and *Barbadoes*, &c. ready bottled, which is commonly ſo ſent from *Herefordſhire* to *London*.

It is ſuppoſed that we may make as good Wines as in *France*, (if Vineyards were planted on the ſides of Hills or Banks, which are defended from the cold North-Weſt Winds) with ſuch Vines as the *French*-men commonly make thoſe Wines of ; for the Climate is as proper as any part of *France*, therefore it is rational to believe, that the Wines will be as rich and good as in *France*, There are ſome Vine-yards already planted in *Pennſylvania*, and more intended to be planted by ſome *French-Proteſtants*, and others, that are gone to ſettle there.

Several other Commodities may be raiſed here, as *Rice*, which is known to have been ſown for a tryal, and it grew very well, and yielded good encreaſe.

Alſo *Annis-Seeds* I have been informed groweth well, and might be a profitable Commodity, there being great Quan-tities uſed in *England* by Diſtillers.

Liquoriſh doubtleſs would grow very well. And I queſtion

ftion not but that *Mather, Woad,* and other Plants and Roots for Dyers ufe might be raifed. *Shuemack* groweth naturally. Alfo feveral ufeful Durgs grow naturally, as *Saffafrafs, Saffaperella, Callamus Aromaticus, Snake-Root, Jallappa,* &c.

The *Pine-Tree* groweth here, out of which is made *Pitch, Tar, Rofin* and *Turpentine:* In *New-England* fome make quantities of *Tar* out of the knots of *Pine Trees,* with which they fupply themfelves and others.

There are many other forts of *Plants, Roots* and *Herbs* of great Virtue, which grow here, which are found to cure fuch Diftempers as the People are infident to.

Hops in fome places grow naturally, but were *Hop*-Gardens planted in low rich Land, quantities might be raifed to good advantage.

There is no *Lime Stone* as we yet know of, but we make *Lime* of *Oyster* Shels, which by the Sea and Bay fide are fo plentiful, that we may load Ships with them.

There are feveral forts of good *Clay,* of which Bricks, Earthen-Ware, and Tobacco-Pipes are made; and in fome places there are Quaries of a ruf hard Stone, which are good to wall Cellars, and fome Stone fit for Pavement.

The *Trees* grow but thin in moft places, and very little under-Wood. In the *Woods* groweth plentifully a courfe fort of *Grafs,* which is fo proving, that it foon makes the Cattel and Horfes fat in the Summer, but the *Hay* being courfe, which is chiefly gotten on the frefh Marfhes, the Cattel lofeth their Flefh in the Winter, and become very poor, except we give them Corn. But this may be remydied in time, by draining of low rich Land, and by plowing of it, and fowing it with *Englifh*-Grafs-feed, which here thrives very well

The *Hogs* are fat in the VVoods when it is a good Maft-Year.

The

The Woods are furnished with ſtore of Wild Fowl, as *Turkeys*, *Pheſants*, *Heath-Cocks*, *Partridges*, *Pidgeons*, *Black-birds*, &c. And People that will take the pains to raiſe the various ſorts of tame Fowl, may do it with as little trouble, and leſs charge, then they can in *England*, by reaſon of what they find in the Woods.

Bees are found by the experience of ſeveral that keep them, to thrive very well.

I do not queſtion but that we might make good ſtrong ſound *Beer*, *Ale* and *Mum*, that would keep well to *Barbadoes*; the Water being good, and *Wheat* and *Barley* in a few Years like to be very plentiful : Great quantities of *Beer*, *Ale* and *Mum* is ſent yearly from *London*, and other places, to *Barbadoes*, *Jamaica*, and other Iſlands in *America*, where it ſells to good advantage ; and if *Beer*, *Ale* and *Mum* hold good from *England* to thoſe places, which 'tis ſaid is above one thouſand Leagues ; I queſtion not but if it be well brewed in a ſeaſonable time of the Year, and put up in good Casks, but it will keep good to be Tranſported from *Delaware* River to thoſe Iſlands aforeſaid, which by computation, is not above half ſo far. If Merchants can gain by ſending *Beer*, *Ale* and *Mum* from *England*, where Corn is dear, and Freight dear, by reaſon of the length of the Voyage, we in all probability muſt get much more, that buy our Corn cheap, and pay leſs Freight.

Flower and *Bisket* may be made in great quantities in a few Years, the Wheat being very good, which ſeldom fails of finding a good Market at *Barbadoes*, *Jamaica*, and the *Carieb* Iſlands : great quantities are ſent yearly from *London*, and other places, which if they can make Profit of it, we much more for the Reaſons already given.

Pork is but about half the price as in *England*, therefore the Inhabitants will ſeldom have their Market ſpoiled by

B　　　　　　　　　　　　　　　any

any that come from *England*, of which Commodity the Inhabitants in a few Years will have Quantities to fell to the Merchant, which is falted, and packed in Barrels, and fo tranf-ported to *Jamaica*, *Barbadoes*, *Nevis*, and other Iflands. Hams of *Bacon* are alfo made, much after the fame manner as in *Weft-Falia*, and the Bacon eats much like it.

Our *Beef* in the Fall is very fat and good, and we are like-ly in a few Years to have great Plenty, which will ferve our Families, and furnifh Shipping.

Our *Mutton* is alfo fat, found and good, being only fed with natural Grafs; but if we fprinkle but a little *Englifh* Hay-Seed on the Land without Plowing, and then feed Sheep on it, in a little time it will fo encreafe, that it will cover the Land with *Englifh* Grafs, like unto our Paftures in *England*, provided the Land be good. We find the Profits of Sheep are confiderable.

Our *Butter* is very good, and our *Cheefe* is indifferent good, but when we have Paftures of *Englifh* Gafs, (which many are getting into) then I fuppofe our *Cheefe* will be as good as that of *England*.

Our *Horfes* are good ferviceable Horfes, fit both for Draught and Saddle, the Planters will ride them fifty Miles a day, without Shoes, and fome of them are indifferent good fhapes; of which many Ships are freighted yearly from *New-England* with Horfes to *Barbadoes*, *Nevis*, and other places; and fome Ships have alfo been freighted out of *Pennfylvania* and *New-Jerfey* with Horfes to *Barbadoes*; but if we had fome choice Horfes from *England*, and did get fome of the beft of our Mares, and keep them well in the Winter, and in Paftures inclofed in the Summer, to prevent there going a-mongft other Horfes, we might then have a choice breed of Horfes, which would tend much to the advantage of the Inhabitants.

The

The Commodities fit to fend to *England*, befides what are already named, are the Skins of the feveral wild Beafts that are in the Country, as *Elks*, *Deer*, *Beaver*, *Fisher*, *Bear*, *Fox*, *Rackoon*, *Marten*, *Otter*, *Woolf*, *Muskquash*, *Mink*, *Cat*, &c.

Potashes may be here made, and *Soap*, not only to the fupply of our felves, but to fell to our Neighbours.

Alfo *Iron* may be here made, there being one *Iron*-Work already in Eaft-*Jerfey*.

Likewife, we may furnifh Merchants with Pipe-Staves, and other Coopers Timber and Hoops.

The *Woolen* Manufacture may be mannaged in *Pennfylvania* and *New-Jerfey*, to good advantage, the upper parts of the Country being very fit for the keeping of Sheep, the Wool being found to be good, and the Sheep not fubject to the *Rot*: The Ewes commonly after the firft time, bring two Lambs at once.

But it may be queried, *How fhall the Sheep be preferved from the Woolf?*

I anfwer; Get fuch a Flock as it may anfwer the charge, for a boy to make it his full Employment to look after them, and let them be pend at Night in a Houfe or Fold provided for that purpofe. If one man have not enough to imploy a Shepherd, then let feveral joyn their Stock together.

But it may be queried, *Where fhall Wool be gotten to carry on the Woollen Manufacture, untill we have of our own raifing?*

I anfwer; in *Road Ifland*, and fome other adjacent Iflands and Places, Wool may be bought at fix Pence a Pound, and confiderable Quantities may be there had, which will fupply until we can raife enough of our own.

Alfo, we may have *Cotton-Wool* from *Barbadoes*, and other adjacent Iflands in returns for our Provifions that we fend them. So that the making of Cotton-Cloth and Fuftians

may

may be likewife made to good advantage, the *Cotten-Wool* being purchafed by the growth of our own Country; and the Linnen-Yarn being fpun by our own Families, of *Flax*, of our own growth and ordering.

The *Tanning*-Trade and *Shoemaking* may be here mannaged to good advantage, *Hides* being plenty, and to be had at moderate Prices, and *Lark* to be had for only the charge in getting it.

A *Skinner* that can drefs Skins in Oyl, may do very well; for we have *Elk* skins, and plenty of *Buck* and *Doe* skins, which the Inhabitants give (at *New-York*, where there are fuch Trades) one half for dreffing the other.

There ought to be *publick Store-Houfes* provided for all Perfons to bring their Flax, Hemp and Linnen Cloth to, where it may be preferved clean and dry at a very fmall Charge, and the owner at liberty to take it out at his own will and pleafure, or to fell, transfer or affign it to any other. Now the Hemp, Flax and Linnen Cloth being brought into the publick Store-Houfe, and the Quantity, Quality and Value of it there regiftred in the Book, to be kept for that purpofe; and the Perfon that hath put in the faid Hemp, Flax and Linnen Cloth, taking a Note under the Hand and Seal, from the Store-houfe Regifter, of the quantity, quality and value of the Hemp Flax, and Linnen Cloth brought into the publick Store-Houfe, with the time it was delivered; thefe Notes will pafs from one man to another all one as Money: *As for Example*, Suppofe I am a Merchant, that am furnifhed with divers forts of goods, I fell them to a Planter, and receive their Notes which they had from the Store-houfe *Regiftry*, in pay for my goods, to the value of one hundred Pounds. I buy of the Clothier in Woolen Cloth to the value of fixty pounds, and of the Roper in Cordage to the value of forty pounds; I pay them by thefe Notes on the Store-houfe; the Clother he buys Woolen Yarn

of

of the Master of the Spinning-School, to the value of sixty
pounds, and payes him by these Notes on the publick Store;
the Master of the Spinning-School buys of the Farmer in
Wool to the value of sixty pounds, and pays him by these
Notes; the Farmer buyeth of the Merchant in Goods to the
value of sixty pounds, and pays him by these Notes; the Merchant receiveth on demand, from the publick Store, in Linnen
Cloth to the value of sixty pound, at receiving thereof he de-
livereth up the Notes to the Register of the publick Store,
which are cancelled, and then filed up as Waste paper. The
Roper, when he pleaseth, receives on demand, in Hemp to
the value of forty pounds out of the publick Store, by which
he is made capable of imploying his Servants in making of
Cordage ; but he that hath no occasion to take out this Hemp
or Flax, or Linnen Cloth, may pass these Notes from one man
to another, as often they please, which is all one as ready
Money at all times.

Were the Flax and Hemp Manufactuaries carried on to that
height as it might be, it would greatly advance these Countries : for did we make our own Sail-cloth and Cordage,
we could make Ships, Sloops and Boats at much easier Rates
than they can build for in *England*, the Timber costing us nothing but Labour. And were more Saw-Mills made (of
which there are divers already) to cut Planks and other Tim-
, both Ships and Houses might be built at easie Rates.

Many Ship Loads of Hemp is brought yearly from the East
Countries to *England*, which is afterward there made into
Cordage, Twine, Sacking, Fishing-Nets &c. and then trans-
ported from thence to *Jamaica, Barbadoes, Virginia, New-
England*, and other parts of *America*, so that doubtless ma-
terials made of Hemp, must be sold in *America* by the Retaler,
at double the price as it cost where it grew ; by which it appears that at those prices we should have double for our labour

bour, to what they have, and our Provisions as Cheap as theirs, it being raised on Land that cost us little.

1. Now It might be well if a Law were made by the Governours and general Assemblies of *Pennsilvania* and *New-Jersey*, that all Persons inhabiting in the said Provinces, do put their Children seven years to the publick School, or longer, if the Parents please.

2. That Schools be provided in all Towns and Cities, and Persons of known honesty, skill and understanding be yearly chosen by the Governour and General Assembly, to teach and instruct Boys and Girls in all the most useful Arts and Sciences that they in their youthful capacities may be capable to understand, as the learning to *Read* and *Write true English, Latine,* and other useful Speeches and Languages, and *fair Writing, Arithmatick* and *Book-keeping*; and the Boys to be taught and instructed in some Mystery or Trade, as the making of *Mathematical Instruments,* Joynery, *Turnery,* the making of *Clocks* and *Watches, Weaving, Shoe-making,* or any other useful Trade or Mystery that the School is capable of teaching; and the Girls to be taught and instructed in *Spinning* of *Flax* and *Wool,* and *Knitting* of *Gloves* and *Stockings, Sewing,* and making of all sorts of useful *Needle Work,* and the making of *Straw-Work,* as *Hats, Baskets, &c.* or any other useful Art or Mystery that the School is capable of teaching.

3. That the Scholars be kept in the Morning two hours at *Reading, Writing, Book-keeping &c.* and other two hours at work in that Art, Mystery or Trade that he or she most delighteth in, and then let them have two hours to dine, and for Recreation; and in the afternoon two hours at *Reading, Writing, &c.* and the other two hours at work at their several Imployments.

4. The seventh day of the Week the Scholars may come to school only in the fore-noon, and at a certain hour in the after-

after-noon let a Meeting be kept by the School-mafters and their Scholars, where after good inftruction and admonition is given by the Mafters, to the Scholars, and thanks returned to the Lord for his Mercies and Bleffings that are daily received from him, then let a ftrict examination be made by the Mafters, of the Converfation of the Scholars in the week paft, and let reproof, admonition and correction be given to the Offendors, according to the quantity and quality of their faults.

5. Let the like Meetings be kept by the School-Miftriffes, and the Girls apart from the Boys. By ftrictly obferving this good Order, our Children will be hindred of running into that Excefs of Riot and Wickednefs that youth is incident to, and they will be a comfort to their tender Parents.

6. Let one thoufand Acres of Land be given and laid out in a good place, to every publick School that fhall be fet up, and the Rent or incom of it to go towards the defraying of the charge of the School.

7. And to the end that the Children of poor People, and the Children of *Indians* may have the like good Learning with the Children of Rich People, let them be maintained free of charge to their Parents, out of the Profits of the fchool, arifing by the Work of the Scholars, by which the Poor and the *Indians*, as well as the Rich, will have their Children taught, and the Remainder of the Profits, if any be, to be difpofed of in the building of School-houfes, and Improvements on the thoufand Acres of Land, which belongs to the School.

The manner and Profits of a *Spinning-School* in *Germany*, as it is laid down by *Andrew Yarenton* in his own words, in a Book of his, call'd, *England's Improvements by Sea and Land*, take as followeth.

'In *Germany*, where the Thred is made that makes the fine 'Linnens, in all Towns there are Schools for little Girls, from 'fix years old, and upwards, to teach them to fpin, and fo to
'bring

' bring their tender fingers by degrees to spin very fine ; their
' Wheels go all by the Foot, made to go with much ease,
' whereby the action or motion is very easie and delightful:
' The way, method, rule and order how they are govern'd is,
' 1st. There is a large Room, and in the middle thereof a little
' Box like a Pulpit : 2dly, There are Benches built round about
' the Room, as they are in Play-houses, upon the benches sit
' about two hundred Children spinning, and in the box
' in the middle of the Room, sits the grand Mistress with a
' long white Wand in her hand ; if she observe any of them
' idle, she reaches them a tap, but if that will not do, she rings
' a bell, which by a little Cord is fixed to the box, and out
' comes a VVoman, she then points to the Offendor, and she
' is taken away into another Room and chastized ; and all
' this is done without one word speaking : In a little Room
' by the School there is a VVoman that is preparing, and put-
' ting Flax on the Distaffs, and upon the ringing of a Bell, and
' pointing the Rod at the Maid that hath spun off her Flax,
' she hath another Distaff given her, and her Spool of Thred
' taken from her, and put into a box unto others of the same
' size, to make Cloth, all being of equal Threds. 1st. They
' raise their Children, as they spin finer, to the higher Benches:
' 2. They sort and size all the Threds, so that they can apply
' them to make equal Cloths; and after a young Maid hath been
' three years in the *Spinning-School*, that is taken in at six, and
' then continues until nine years, she will get eight pence the
' day, and in these parts I speak of, a man that has most
' Children, lives best

Now were *Spining-Schools* settled in the principal Cities and
Towns in *Pennsyvania* and *New-Jersey*, and a Law made to
oblige the Parents of Children, to put their Children to
school, we should then soon come into such a way of making
Linnen-Cloth, as that we should not only have sufficient fo
ou

our own supply, but also should have quantities to sell to the Inhabitants of our own neighbouring Provinces, where it will sell at considerable Prices, they being usually supplied from *England*, where it must be dear, after Freight, Custom, and other charges at Importation, with the Merchants profit considered; and yet nevertheless th s Cloth, thus dear bought will sell in *New-England, Virginia,* and some other places in *America,* at thirty Pound *per Cent* profit, above the first cost in *England,* and the Moneys paid by Bills of Exchange, and the Retailer makes commonly on Goods thus bought not less then twenty Pounds *per Cent.* profit : So that if all things be considered, the Cloth is sold in *America,* to the Planter at full double the price as it cost from the maker in *France* or *Germany,* from whence its brought to *England,* by which it doth appear, that if we do get such Prices for the Cloth that we make, then we shall have double for our Labour to what they have ; therefore it may be well that a Law were made for the encouragement of the *Linnen Manufacture* by the Governours and General Assemb'ies, that all Persons inhabiting in *Pennsylvania,* or *New-Jersey,* that keep a Plow, do sow one Acre of *Flax,* and two Acres of *Hemp,* which would be a means of supplying us with *Flax* and *Hemp,* to carry on the Manufacturies of *Linnen-Cloth* and *Cordage* ; and also would be very profitable to the Planter, by imploying his Family in the Winter season, when they would have otherwise but little else to do, *viz.* the Men and Boys in Breaking and Dressing of it, and making it fit for use, and the Women and Girls in Spining it, and nevertheless they may carry on their Husbandry as largely, as if nothing of this was done ; the Husbandry-Affairs being chiefly betwixt the Spring and Fall.

Now to that end that a *Bank* of *Monies* and *Credit* may be in *Pennsilvania* and *New-Jersey,* a Law may be made, that all

C

Monies

Monies lent on Interest be at 8 l. per Cent. by the year, and that all Bills and Bonds be entred on the publick Registry, and by Act of Assembly be made transferable by Assignments, so as the Property may go along with the Assignment ; thereby a Bond or Bill will go in the nature of Bills of Exchange ; and so A. owing 200 l. to B. he assigns him the Bond of C. who owed him 200 l. and C. owing D. 200 l. assigns him the Bond of E. who owed him 200 l. and so one Bond or Bill would go through twenty hands, and thereby be as ready Monies, and do much to the Benefit of Trade. Also, that all Lands and Houses be put under a publick Registry, and entred in the Book, with an account of the value of them, and how occupied and tenanted, a particular thereof being given under the Hand and Seal of the Office to the Owners. We having thus fitted our selves with a publick Registry of all our Lands and Houses, whereby it is made ready Money at all times, without the charge of Law, or the necessity of a Lawyer ; and a Law being made for the payment of such large Interest for Monies lent, and the security being so undeniably good, a Bank will in time arise, and such a Bank as will be for the benefit and advantage of Pennsilvania and New-Jersey, and Trade universal.

Suppose my self, and some others have in Houses and Lands in Pennsilvania or New-Jersey, worth 3000 l. and are minded to mannage and carry on the Linnen Manufacture, but cannot do it, without borrowing on Interest 2000 l. therefore we come to the Bank in Pennsilvania or New Jersey, and there tender a particular of our Lands and Houses, and how occupied or tennanted, being worth 3000 l. in Pennsilvania or New-Jersey, and desire them to lend us 2000 l. and we will Mortgage our Land & Houses for it ; the answer will be, We will send to the Register's Office your particular, and at the return of the Messenger you shall have your answer : The

Registers

Registers send answer, it is our Lands and Houses, and occupied, and tenanted, and valued according to the particular, there needs no more words but to tell us the Money, with which we carry on the Trade briskly, to the great benefit and advantage of some hundreds of People that we set to work, and to the supplying of the Inhabitants with Cloth made of Flax, grown, drest, spun and wove in our own Provinces; which Trade we could not mannage and carry on without this credit, but having this credit, we go on with our Trade comfortably, and the Lender will have his ends answered, and his Moneys well secured. And its certain, such an Anchorage, Fund, and Foundation, will then bring out the Monyes unimployed from all Persons in these Provinces, even People of all degrees will put in their Monyes, which will be put out again into Trade to Merchants, and such as stand in need of ready Monyes; and thereby Trade is made easie, and much convenienced.

Suppose ten Families purchase in *Pennsilvania* or *New-Jersey* five thousand Acres of Land, and they lay out a small Township in the middle of it, for the conveniency of neighbourhood, to each Family one hundred Acres for Houses, Gardens, Orchards, Corn-fields and Pastures of English Grass, the remainder to lie in common, to feed their Cattel; and suppose that by that time they have built their dwelling Houses, Cow-houses, Barnes, and other Out-houses, and have made Inclosures about their home-lots, that their Monyes is all expended, and without a further supply to buy Oxen and Horses to plow their Land, and Cows to find their Families in Milk, Butter and Cheese, and Sows to breed a stock on, they will live but meanly for some time, therefore to amend their condition they come to the Bank, and there tender a particular of their Lands, valued to be worth 1500 *l.* on which they desire to take up 1000 *l.* to purchase a Stock of Oxen, Horses, Cows, Sows, Sheep and Servants, by which they will be en-

abled

abled to carry on their Husbandry to great advantage, and the
benefit of the Province in general; and it may be that in two
or three years time, they may be able to pay in this Money,
with Interest, to the owner; and in two or three years more
may be able to bring into the Bank, to be lent out to others,
one thousand pounds of their own Estates.

As to the benefit of **publick Granaries** on *Delaware River*,
to keep the Corn for all Merchants, Bakers and Farmers that
please to send it thither, that so the destruction and damages
occasioned by Rats and Mice, may be prevented. In this Granary, Corn at all times may be taken in, from all Persons that
please to send it, and the Corn so sent may be preserved sweet,
safe, and in good Order, at a small charge for a whole year,
and the owner at liberty to take it out at his own will and
pleasure, or to sell, transfer or assign any part of the said Corn
to any Person or Persons for the payment of his Debts, or to
furnish himself with Clothing, or other Necessaries from the
Merchant; and the Granary-keepers to give good security
that all things should be faithfully done & discharged. Now
the Corn being brought into the publick Granary, and there
registred in the Register-Book, to be kept for that purpose;
and the Person that hath put in the said Corn, taking a Note
under hand and seal, from the Granary-Register, of the quantity of Corn brought into the Granary, with the time it was
delivered, and the matter and kind of the Corn, then these
Advantages will ensue:

First, Preservation from the Rats and Mice, Straw to supply
his Cattel, the Chaff for his Horses, and the light Corn to feed
his Pigs and Poultry; his Husbandry mannaged with rule and
order to his advantage; no forc'd haste, but thrashing and
carrying the Corn to the Granary in times wherein his servants
have leisure; so in seeding time & harvest all People are freed
from that. Besides, there being at all times sufficient quantities

ties of Corn in the Granaries to load Ships, Merchants from *Barbadoes*, and other places, will come to buy Corn; of one Farmer he may buy one hundred Bushels, of another fifty, and so he may buy the Corn that belongs to sixty or eighty Farmers, and receive their Notes which they had from the Granary-Office, which Corn he letteth lie in the Granary until he have occasion to use it, then he orders his Baker to go with those notes to the Granary-Office, and receive such quantities as he hath a mind shall be made into Flower and Bisket, which the Baker does accordingly, and gets it packt up in Casks, and sent to *Barbadoes*; the remainder, if he please, he may sell to some other Merchant that lives at *Barbadoes*, or some other place, and when sold, may deliver the said Merchant the Notes on the Granary-Office, at sight whereof they may receive their Corn, if they please, or they may pass those Notes from one to another, as often as they please, which is all one as Money, the Corn being lodged safe, and kept in the publick Granary, will be the occasion of imploying much of the Cash of *Pennsilvania* and *New-Jersey*; most People near these publick Bank-Granaries, will be dealing to have some Corn in Bank-Credit; for that cannot miss of finding an encrease and benefit to them in the rise of Corn.

The best places at present for the building of *Granaries*, are, I suppose, *Burlington* in *West-Jersey*, *Philadelphia* and *New-Castle* in *Pennsilvania*, and *New Perth* in *East-Jersey*, which places are excellently situated, there being many Navigable Rivers, whereby Trade is very communicable, and the Corn may be brought in Boats and Sloops from most places now inhabited, by water to these publick Granaries, for small charge, and from the Granaries may be carried to Water-Mills to grind, which are some of them so conveniently situated, that Boats may come to the Mill-Tayl, which is also a great conveniency to those that trade much in Corn.

Now

Now I will demonftrate, and fhew you the length,
breadth and heighth the *Granaries* ought to be of, to hold
this Corn; as alfo the Charge of building one of them, and
the way how it fhould be built for the beft advantage, with
the way of ordering and managing the Corn, that it may
keep good, fweet and clean, eight or ten Years. The *Granaries* muft be three hundred Foot long, eighten Foot wide
betwixt infide and infide, feven Stories high, each Story
feven Foot high, all to be built of good well burnt Brick, and
laid in Lime and Sand very well; the ends of the *Granaries*
muft be fet *North* and *South*, fo the fides will be *Eaft* and
Weft; and in the fides of the *Granaries*, there muft be large
Windows to open and fhut clofe, that when the Wind blows
at *Weft*, the Windows may be laid open, and then the *Granary* man will be turning and winding the Corn, and all
Filth and Drofs will be blown out at the Window. When
the Weather is fair, then throw open the Windows, to let
in the Air to the Corn; and in the middle, there muft be
Stoves to be kept with Fire in them in all moift or wet times,
or at going away of great *Frofts* and *Snows*, to prevent moift-
nefs either in the Brick-walls, Timber, Boards or Corn.
There muft be in each fide of the *Granaries*, three or four long
Troughs or Spouts fixt in the uppermoft Loft, which muft
run about twenty Foot out of the *Granary*; and in fine
Weather, the *Granary* men muft be throwing the Corn out
of the uppermoft Loft, and fo it will fall into another Spout
made ten Foot wide at the top, and through that Spout the
Corn defcends into the lowermoft Loft, and then wound up
on the infide of the *Granary*, by a Crane fixt for that purpofe,
and the Corn receiving the benefit of the Air, falling down
thirty Foot before it comes into the fecond Spout, cleanfeth
it from its filth and Chaff; thefe Spouts are to be taken off
and on, as occafion requires, and to be fixt to another of the
Lofts

Lofts, that when Veſſels come to load Corn, they may through theſe Spouts convey the Corn into the Boats or Sloops, without any thing of Labour, by carrying it on the Backs of men.

The charge of one *Granary* three Hundred Foot long, eighteen Foot wide, ſeven Stories high, ſeven Foot betwixt each Story, being built with Brick in *England*, as by the Account of *Andrew Tarenton*, take as followeth; *Six hundred thouſand of Bricks builds a* Granary, *two Bricks and a half thick the two firſt Stories, two Bricks thick the three next Stories, Brick and a half thick the two uppermoſt Stories; and the Brick will be made and delivered on the Place for eight Shillings the Thouſand, the laying of Brick three Shillings the Thouſand, Lime and Sand two Shillings the Thouſand; ſo Brick-laying, Lime and Sand will be thirteen Shillings the Thouſand, one hundred and fifty Tuns of Oak for Summers-Joiſts and Roof,* 170 l. *Boards for the ſix Stories, ſixty thouſand Foot, at* 13 s. 4 d. *The one hundred Foot and ten thouſand Foot for Window-Doors and Spouts at the ſame rate,* 48 l. *Laths and Tiles* 100 l. *Carpenters work* 70 l. *Iron, Nails, and odd things* 60 l. *So the charge of a Granary will be* 800 l. *There will be kept in this* Granary *fourteen thouſand Quarters of Corn, which is two thouſand Quarters in every Loft, which will be a thouſand Buſhels in every Bay; ſix labouring men, with one Clerk, will be ſufficient to manage this* Granary, *to turn and wind the Corn, and keep the Books of Accounts; fifteen pounds a piece allowed to the ſix men, and thirty pound a year to the Clark or Regiſter, will be Wages ſufficient; ſo the Servants Wages will be* 120 l. per annum; *allow ten in the hundred for Monies laid out for building the* Granaries, *which is* 80 l. *ſo the charge will be yearly* 200 l. *Now if the Country-man pay ſix pence a Quarter yearly for keeping his Corn ſafe and ſweet in the Granary, fourteen thouſand Quarters will come to* 350 l. *for Granary-Rent yearly.*

Admit

Admit I have a Propriety of Land in *Pennſilvania* or *New-Jerſey*, either place then alloweth me to take up five thouſand Acres, with Town or City-Lots, upon condition that I ſettle ten Families on it, therefore I ſend over ten Families of honeſt induſtrous People, the charge of each Family is 100 *l.* as by the account of particulars appears, as followeth.

	l.	*s.*	*d.*
For one hundred Acres of Land,	05	00	00
For the Paſſage of the Family, five perſons,	25	00	00
For freſh proviſions to uſe on Ship board, over and above the Ships allowances, as *Rice, Oatmeal, Flower, Butter, Sugar, Brandy*, and ſome odd things more, which I leave to the diſcretion of thoſe that go,	05	00	00
For 3 hundred weight of ſix penny, eight penny and ten penny Nails, to be uſed on ſides and Roof of the Houſe,	05	00	00
For a Share and Coulter, a Plow-Chain, 2 Sythes, 4 Sickles, a horſe Collar, ſome Cordage for Harneſs, 2 Stock Locks, 2 weeding Hoes, 2 grubbing Hoes, one croſs-cut Saw, 2 Iron Wedges, 1 Iron Pot, 1 frying Pan, 2 falling Axes, 1 broad Ax, 1 Spade, 1 Hatchet, 1 Fro to cleave Clapboard, Shingle and Coopers Timber,	05	00	9
For Portridge, Cuſtom-houſe charge and fraight, &c. on the goods,	02	00	00
For Inſurance of the one hundred pound	03	00	00
In all	50	00	00

The remaining fifty Pounds may do well to lay out in theſe goods, which are the moſt vendable in the Country, *viz.*

Ten

	l.	*s.*	*d.*
Ten pieces of Serge, at	20	00	00
Six pieces of narrow blew Linnen, containing about seven hundred Yards,	05	00	00
200 Ells of brown Offembrigs, at about	07	10	00
Half a piece of three quarters Dowlis,	03	10	00
Three pieces of coulered Linnen	02	10	00
Two pieces of Yorkſhire Kerſeys,	04	00	00
One piece of red Peniſton, above 40 yards, at 18 d, per Yard,	03	00	00
One piece of Demity,	00	15	00
In Buttons and Silk, Tape and Thred ſuitable to the Clothes,	03	15	00
In All	50	00	00

And when you come into the Country, you may lay out the above-mentioned goods to purchaſe a ſtock of Cattel and Proviſions, *&c.* which for goods at the firſt coſt in *England,* will buy at the prices under-mentioned, *viz.*

	l.	*s.*	*d.*
One pair of working Oxen, at	60	00	00
One Mare 3 *l.* and four Cows and Calves, 12 *l.*	15	00	00
One Bull 2 *l.* ten Ewes 3 *l.* 10 *s.*	05	10	00
Four breeding Sows, and one Boor,	04	00	00
One fat Ox to kill for winter Proviſions,	03	10	00
400 pound of Pork, at 3 half pence *per pound,*	02	10	00
24 pound of Butter, at 4 *d.* *per pound,*	00	08	00
One Barrel of ſalted Fiſh,	00	10	00
One Barrel of Malaſſas to make Beer,	01	08	00
40 Buſhels of Indian Corn, at 1 *s.* 8 *d.* *per Buſhel,*	03	06	08
20 Buſhels of Rye, at 2 *s.* *per Buſhel,*	02	00	00
20 Buſhels of Wheat, at 3 *s* *per Buſhel,*	03	00	00
6 Buſhels of Peaſe and Indian Beans, *per* Buſhel,	00	18	00
2 Buſhels of Salt, at 2 *s.* *per Buſhel,*	00	04	00
50 pound of Cheeſe of the Country-making, at 3 *d.* *per pound,*	00	12	06
12 pound of Candles, at 5 *d.* *per pound,*	00	05	00
In Sugar, Spice, and other things,	00	17	10
In All	50	00	00

D

Note, That the above-mentioned Prices is for goods at firſt
coſt in England, which in Country Money would be ſome-
thing above one third higher, *viz.* a Cow and Calf valued
in goods at firſt coſt at 3 *l.* is worth in Country Money 5 *l.*
and other things advance much after the ſame proportion.

My five thouſand Acres of Land coſt me 100 *l.* I had of
the ten Families for the one thouſand Acres diſpoſed of to
them 50 *l.* my Town or City Lots will yield me currant 50 *l.*
by which it appears I am nothing out on the four thouſand
Acres that is left.

I get my five thouſand Acres ſurveyed and laid out to me,
out of which I lay out for the ten Families one thouſand Acres,
which may be ſo divided, as that each family may live near
one to the other; I intend with them to let the Money lie in
their hands ſix years, for which they to pay me each family,
8 *l.* a year, in conſideration of the one hundred pound a family laid out for them, and at the expiration of the ſix years,
they to pay me my 1000 *l.* viz. each family 100 *l.* as by agreement; my Money being paid me, I am unwilling to let it lie
dead, therefore I lay out in the middle of my Land one thouſand Acres, which I divide into ten lots, in form and manner
as before, then I intend, with fifty Servants to ſerve me four
years a piece, I place them on the Land, *viz.* five on each lot.
Their Paſſage, and in goods to purchaſe Cattel and Proviſions,
&c. is to each five ſervants 100 *l.* as before is explained; Now
I order a Houſe to be built, and Orchards, Gardens and In-
cloſures to be made, and Husbandry affairs to be carried on on
each lot; ſo that at the four years end, as the ſervants time is
expired, I ſhall have ten Farms, each containing four hundred Acres; for the one thouſand Acres being laid out in the
middle of my Land, the remaining three thouſand Acres
joyns to it.

My

My servants time being expired, I am willing to see what charge I am out upon these ten Farms and Stock, in order to know what I have gain'd in the ten years past, over and above 8 *l. per Cent. Interest*, that is allowed me for the use of my Money: I am out by the first charge 1000 *l.* & the Interest thereof for four years, at 8 *l. per Cent.* is for the four years 320 l. so that the whole charge on the ten Farms, Principal & Interest, comes to 1320 l. Now if I value my ten Farms but at 400 l. each, which is 20 *s. per Acre*, one with another ; then the whole will be 4000 l. besides the first Stock of Cattel and Hogs, &c to each Plantation, with its Increase for four years, which Stock cost at first to each Farm 30 *l.* in goods at first cost, but is worth 40 *l.* sterling, at which rate the Stock on the ten Farms cost 400 *l.* and if we account the four years Increase to be no more than the first Stock, yet that is 400 *l.* by which it appears that the ten Farms, and the stock on them is worth 4800 *l.* out of which deduct the Money laid out, which with Interest is 1320 *l.* So the the Neat profit, besides 8 *l. per Cent.* allowed for Interest, is for this ten years improvement, 3480 *l.* and twenty Families set at liberty from that extream Slavery that attended them, by reason of great Poverty that they endured in *England*, and must have so continued, had not they been thus redeemed by coming into *America*. It may be thought that this is too great an undertaking for one man, which if it be, then I propose that ten joyn together in this community, and each man send over five Servants, of which let one of them be an honest man that understands Country business, as an Overseer, which if we allow him over and above his Passage and Diet 20 *l.* a year for his four years service, this amounts to 80 *l.* which is for the ten farms 800 *l.* which being deducted out of the 3480 *l.* there only remains 2680 *l.* clear profit to the ten men, which is for each man 268 *l.* for his ten years improvement of his 100 *l.* and his 100 *l.* back

again

again with Interest for all the time at 8 *l. per Cent. per annum,* the whole producing 448 *l.* for his 100 *l.* first laid out.

Some may object, and say, *They cannot believe the Land of each farm, with its Improvements, will sell at* 20 s. *an Acre, that is, at twelve years purchase* 1 s. 8 d. *per Acre per annum. because three hundred Acres of it is as it was,* viz. Rough Woods.

I *Answer;* That although it be so, yet these Woods are made valuable by the twenty Families that are seated near them, the first ten families having been settled ten years, the last four years; for some are willing to have their Children live near them; and and they having but one hundred Acres in all, it will not be well to divide that, therefore they will give a good price for one hundred Acres, to settle a Child upon, to live by them, as experience sheweth; for in *Rhode-Island,* which is not far from us, Land rough in the Woods, not better than ours, will sell at 40 s. an Acre, which is 3 s. 4 d. *per Acre per annum.* Therefore, Reader, I hope now thou art convinced that there is a probability that what I here inform thee of, will prove true, casualties of Fire, &c. excepted.

The *Indians* are but few in Number, and have been very serviceable to us by selling us Venison, *Indian* Corn, Pease and Beans, Fish and Fowl, *Buck* Skins, *Beaver, Otter,* and other Skins and Furs; the Men hunt, Fish and Fowl, and the Women plant the Corn, and carry Burthens; they are many of them of a good Understanding, considering their Education; and in their publick Meetings of Business, they have excellent Order, one speaking after another, and while one is speaking all the rest keep silent, and do not so much as whisper one to the other: We had several Meetings with them, one was in order to put down the sale of *Rum, Brandy,* and other strong Liquors to them, they being a People that have not Government of themselves, so as to drink it in moderation,

ration; at which time there were eight Kings,(& many other *Indians*) one of the was *Ockanickon*, whose dying Words I writ from his Mouth, which you shall have in its order.

The *Indian* Kings sate on a Form, and we sate on another over against them; they had prepared four Belts of *Wampum*, (so their current Money is called, being Black and White *Beads* made of a Fish Shell) to give us as Seals of the Covenant they made with us; one of the Kings by the consent and appointment of the rest stood up and made this following Speech ; *The strong Liquors was first sold us by the* Dutch, *and they were blind, they had no Eyes, they did not see that it was for our hurt ; and the next People that came amongst us, were the* Sweeds, *who continued the sale of those strong Liquors to us : they were also Blind, they had no Eyes, they did not see it to be hurtful to us to drink it, although we know it to be hurtful to us ; but if People will sell it us, we are so in love with it, that we cannot forbear it ; when we drink it, it makes us mad ; we do not know what we do, we then abuse one another ; we throw each other into the Fire, seven Score of our People have been killed, by reason of the drinking of it, since the time it was first sold us : Those People that sell it, they are blind, they have no Eyes, but now there is a People come to live amongst us, that have Eyes, they see it to be for our Hurt, and we know it to be for our Hurt : They are willing to deny themselves of the Profit of it for our good ; these People have Eyes ; we are glad such a People are come amongst us. We must put it down by mutual consent ; the Cask must be sealed up, it must be made fast, it must not leak by Day nor by Night, in the Light, nor in the Dark, and we give you these four Belts of* Wampam, *which we would have you lay up safe, and keep by you to be Witness of this Agreement that we make with you ; and we would have you tell your Children, that these four Belts of* Wampam *are given you to be Witness betaixt us and you of this Agreement.*

A

A Letter from New-Jerſey *in* America *to a Friend in* London.

Dear Friend ;

I Having this ſhort opportunity, have nothing to preſent thee with, but the Dying-Words of an *Indian* King, who died in *Burlington*, and was buried amongſt Friends according to his deſire ; and at his Burial many Tears were ſhed both by the *Innians* and *Engliſh* ; ſo in Love, and great haſte, I reſt thy Friend,
John Cripps.

The Dying-Words of Ockanichon, *ſpoken to* Jachkurſoe, *whom he appointed King after him, ſpoken in the Preſence of ſeveral, who were Eye and Ear Witneſſes of the Truth thereof.*

IT was my deſire, that my Brother's Son, *Jahkurſoe* ſhould be ſent for to come to me to hear my laſt Words, whom I have appointed King after me. My Brother's Son, this day I deliver my Heart into thy Boſom, and would have thee love that which is Good, and to keep good Company, and to refuſe that which is Evil; and to avoid bad Company. Now inaſmuch as I have delivered my Heart into thy Boſom I alſo deliver my Boſom to keep my Heart therein ; therefore alwayes be ſure to walk in a good Path, and never depart out of it. And if any *Indians* ſhould ſpeak any evil of *Indians* or *Chriſtians,* do not joyn with it, but to look to that which is Good, and to joyn with the ſame alwayes. Look at the Sun from the Riſing of it to the Setting of the ſame. In Speeches that ſhall be made between the *Indians* and *Chriſtians,* if any thing be ſpoke that is evil, do not joyn with that, but joyn with that which is good ; and when Speeches are made, do not thou ſpeak firſt, but let all ſpeak before thee,
and

and take good notice what each man speaks, and when thou haſt heard all, joyn to that which is good. Brother's Son, I would have thee to cleanſe thy Ears, and take all Darkneſs and Foulneſs out, that thou mayſt take notice of that which is Good and Evil, and then to joyn with that which is Good, and refuſe the Evil; and alſo to cleanſe thy Eyes, that thou mayeſt ſee both Good and Evil; and if thou ſee any Evil, do not joyn with it, but joyn to that which is Good. Brother's Son, Thou haſt heard all that is paſt; now I would have thee to ſtand up in time of *Speeches*, and to ſtand in my *Steps*, and follow my *Speeches* as I have ſaid before thee, then what thou doſt deſire in Reaſon will be granted thee. Why ſhouldſt thou not follow my Example, inaſmuch as I have had a mind to do that which is Good, and therefore do thou alſo the ſame? Whereas *Sehoppy* and *Swanpis* were appointed Kings by me in my ſtead, and I underſtanding by my Doctor, that *Sehoppy* ſecretly adviſed him not to cure me, and they both being with me at *John Hollinſhead's* Houſe, there I my ſelf ſee by them that they were given more to *Drink*, than to take notice of my *laſt Words*, for I had a mind to make a Speech to them, and to my Brethren the *Engliſh Commiſſioners*, therefore I refuſed them to be Kings after me in my ſtead, and have choſen my Brother's Son *Jahkuroſoe* in their ſtead to ſucceed me.

Brother's Son, I deſire thee to be plain and fair with all, both *Indians* and *Chriſtians*, as I have been. I am very weak, otherwiſe I would have ſpoken more; and in Teſtimony of the Truth of this, I have hereunto ſet my Hand.

The Mark ꝝ of *Ockanickon*, King, now deceaſed.

Henry Jacob Falekinbery, Intrepreter.

Friendly

Friendly Reader, when *Ockanickon* had given his Brothers Son this good Counſel, I thought meet to ſpeak unto him as followeth ; *There is a great God, who Created all thing, and this God giveth Man an underſtanding of what is Good, and what is Bad, and after this Life rewardeth the Good with Bleſſings, and the Bad according to their Doings* ; to which he anſwered and ſaid, *It is very true, it is ſo, there are two Wayes, a broad Way, and a ſtrait Way* ; *there be two Paths, a broad Path and a ſtrait Path* ; *the worſt, and the greateſt Number go in the broad Path, the beſt and feweſt go in the ſtrait Path.*

T. B.

Something in Relation to a Conference had with the Indians *at* Burlington, *ſhortly after we came into the Country.*

THE *Indians* told us, they were adviſed to make War on us, and cut us off whilſt we were but few, and ſaid, They were told, that we ſold them the *Small-Pox,* with the Mach Coat they had bought of us, which cauſed our People to be in Fears and Jealouſies concerning them ; therefore we ſent for the *Indian* Kings, to ſpeak with them, who with many more *Indians,* came to *Burlington,* where we had Conference with them about the matter, therefore told them, That we came amongſt them by their own conſent, and had bought the Land of them, for which we had honeſtly paid them for, and for what Commodities vve had bought at any time of them, vve had paid them for, and had been juſt to them, and had been from the time of our firſt coming very kind and reſpectful to them, therefore vve knevv no Reaſon that they had to make War on us ; to vvhich one of them, in the behalf of the reſt, made this follovving Speech in anſvver, ſaying, 'Our Young Men may ſpeak ſuch Words as vve do
' not

' not like, nor approve of, and vve cannot help that: And
' fome of your Young Men may fpeak fuch Words as you
' do not like, and you cannot help that. We are your Bro-
' thers, and intend to live like Brothers with you : We have
' no mind to have War, for when vve have War, vve are on-
' ly Skin and Bones; the Meat that vve eat doth not do us
' good, vve alvvayes are in fear, vve have not the benefit of
' the Sun to fhine on us, vve hide us in Holes and Corners;
' vve are minded to live at Peace : If vve intend at any time to
' make War upon you, vve vvill let you knovv of it, and the
' Reafons vvhy vve make War vvith you ; and if you make us
' fatisfaction for the Injury done us, for vvhich the War is in-
' tended, then vve vvill not make War on you. And if you
' intend at any time to make War on us, vve vvould have you
' let us knovv of it, and the Reafons for vvhich you make
' VVar on us, and then if vve do not make fatisfaction for
' the Injury done unto you, then you may make VVar on
' us, othervvife you ought not to do it. You are our Bro-
' thers, and vve are vvilling to live like Brothers vvith you :
' We are willing to have a *broad Path* for you and us to walk
' in, and if an *Indian* is afleep in this *Path,* the *Englifh*-man
' fhall pafs him by, and do him no harm; and if an *Englifh*-man
' is afleep in this *path,* the *Indian* fhall pafs him by, and fay, *He*
' *is an Englifh-man, he is afleep, let him alone, he loves to Sleep.* It
' fhall be a *plain Path,* there muft not be in this *path* a *ftump* to
' hurt our *feet.* And as to the *Small-Pox,* it was once in my
' *Grandfathers* time, and it could not be the *Englifh* that could
' fend it us then, there being no *Engiifh* in the Country, and it
' was once in my *Fathers* time, they could not fend it us then
' neither ; and now it is in my time, I do not bclieve that they
' have fent it us now : I do believe it is the Man above that
' hath fent it us.

Some are apt to ask, How we can propose safely to live amongst such a Heathen Poople as the Indians, whose Principles and Practices leads them to War and Bloodshed, and our Principles and Practices leading us to love Enemies, and if reviled, not to revile again ; and if smitten on the one cheek to turn the other, and we being a peaceable People, whose Principles and Practices are against Wars and Fightings ?

I Answer : That we settled by the Indians consent and good liking, and bought the Land of them, that we settle on, which they conveyed to us by Deed under their Hands and Seals, and also submitted to several Articles of agreement with us, viz. **Not to do us any Injury**; but if it should so happen, that any of their People at any time should injure or do harm to any of us, then they to make us satisfaction for the Injury done ; therefore if they break these Covenants and Agreements, then they may be proceeded against as other Offendors, *viz.* to be kept in subjection to the Magistrates Power, in whose hand the Sword of Justice is committed to be used by him, for the punishment of Evil-doers, and praise of them that do well ; therefore I do believe it to be both lawful and expedient to bring Offendors to Justice by the power of the Magistrates Sword, which is not to be used in vain, but may be used against such as raise Rebellions and Insurrections against the Government of the Country, be they *Indians* or others, otherwise it is in vain for us to pretend to Magistracy or Government, it being that which we own to be lawful both in Principle and Practice.

Q. Whether there be not Bears, Wolves, and other Ravenous Beasts in the Country ?

I Answer : Yes. But I have travell'd alone in the Country some hundreds of Miles, and by missing of my way have lain in the Woods all night, and yet I never saw any of those Creatures, nor have I heard that ever man, woman or child were

hurt

hurt by them, they being afraid of Mankind ; also, encouragement is given to both *Indians* and others to kill Wolves, they being paid for every Wolfs head that they bring to the Magiftrate, the value of ten Shillings; and the Bears the *Indians* kill for the profit of their Skins, and fake of their Flesh, which they eat, and efteem better than Deers flesh.

Q. Whether there be not Snakes, more especially the Rattle-Snake ?

Anf. Yes, but not many Rattle-Snakes, and they are eafily difcovered ; for they commonly lie in the Paths for the benefit of the Sun, & if any Perfon draws nigh them, they fhake their Tail, on which the Rattles grow, which make a noife like a childs Rattle ; I never heard of but one Perfon bitten in *Pennfilvania* or *New-Jerfey* with the Rattle-Snake, and he was helpt of it by live Chickens flit affunder and apply'd to the place, which drew out the Poyfon; and as to the other Snake, the moft plentiful is a black Snake, its bite, 'tis faid, does no more harm than the prick of a Pin.

I have mentioned before, that there are a fort of troublefom Flies call'd *Musketoes* (much like the Gnats in *England*) in the lower parts of the Country, where the great Marfhes are, but in the upper parts of the Country feldom one is feen.

There are Crows and Black-birds, which may be accounted amongft the inconveniences, they being deftructive to the *Indian Corn*, the Crows by picking up the Corn juft as its appearing in the blade above ground, and the Black-birds by eating it in the Year, before it be full hard, if not prevented by looking after; but other forts of Corn they feldom hurt.

It is rational to believe, that all confiderate Perfons will fit down and count the coft before they begin to build ; for they muft expect to pafs through a Winter before a Summer, but not fo troublefom a Winter as many have imagined ;for thofe that come there to fettle now, may purchafe Corn, Cattel, and

and other things at the prices mentioned, and may have Houses in some of the Towns of *Pennsilvania* and *New-Jesey* on Rent, until they build for themselves, and Water-Mills to grind their Corn, which are such conveniences that we that went first partly missed of.

Thus, Kind Reader, *I have given thee a true Description of* Pennsilvania *and* New-Jersey, *with the* Rivers *and* Springs, Fish *and* Fowle, Beasts, Fruits, Plants, Corn *and* Commodities *that it doth or may produce, with several other things needful for thee to know, as vvell* Inconveniences *as* Conveniences, *by vvhich I keep clear of that just Reflection of such as are more apt to see faults in others, than to amend them in themselves.*

T. B.

WHereas I unadvisedly published in Print a *Paper*, dated the 13th of *July*, 1685. entituled, *A true and perfect Account of the disposal of the one hundred Shares or Proprieties of the Province of West* New-Jersey, *by* Edward Bylling : In which *Paper* I gave an Account of the purchasers Names, and the several Proprieties granted to them, part of which I took from the Register, the remainder from a List given in by *Edward Bylling*, to the Proprioters, as mentioned on the said *Paper*, which *Paper* I find hath proved Injurious to the aforesaid *Edward Bylling*, although not so intended by me. Therefore in order to give him Satisfaction, and all others that are concerned, I do acknowledge he hath, since the publishing of that *Paper*, shewed me some Deeds, wherein he hath several Proprieties conveyed back to him again, from the original Purchasers and Judge, he may make good Titles to the same.

A

A Letter by Thomas Budd, *sent to his Friends in* Pennsilvania *and* New=Jersey.

Dear Friends ;

YOu are often in my Remembrance, and at this time I feel the tender Bowels of our heavenly Father's Love flowing in my Heart towards you, in a fence of thofe great Exercifes that many of you have, do and may meet vvithal in your *Spiritual Travel* tovvards the *Land of Promife.*

I am alfo fenfible of the many *Exercifes* and invvard *Combats* that many of you met vvithal, after you felt an inclination in your Hearts of Tranfplanting your felves into *America* : Oh the *Breathings* and fervent *Prayers,* and earneft *Defires* that vvere in your Hearts to the Lord, *That you might not go except it was his good Pleafure to remove you, for a purpofe of his own* : This you earneftly defired to be fatisfied in, and many of you received fatisfaction, that it was your places to leave your Native Country, Trades, and near and dear Relations and Friends to tranfplant your felves into a Wildernefs, where you expected to meet with many Tryals and Exercifes of a differing kind, than what you had met withal in your Native Country ; but this you contentedly gave up to, but not without earneft defire, and fervent Prayers to the Lord for his Wifdom to govern you, and his Fatherly Care to preferve you, and his comfortable prefence to be with you, to ftrengthen and enable you chearfuly to undergo thofe new and unaccuftomed Tryals and Exercifes, that you were fenfible would attend you in this weighty undertaking, the Lord heard your Prayers, and anfwered your Defires, inafmuch as that his Fatherly Care was over you, and his living Prefence
did

did accompany you over the great Deep; so that you saw his wonderful Deliverence, and in a sence thereof, you praised his Name for the same.

The Lord having thus far answered our Souls desire, as to bring us to our desired Port in safety, and to remain with us, to be a Counsellor of good things unto us, let us now answer this Kindness unto us by a *righteous Conversation*, and a *pure*, *holy* and *innocent Life*, that others beholding the same, may be convinced thereby, and may glorifie our heavenly Father.

The Eyes of many are on us, some for Good, and some for Evil; therefore my earnest Prayers are to the Lord, That he would preserve us, and give us *Wisdom*, that we may be governed aright before him, and that he would give a good Understanding to those that are in Authority amongst us, that his Law may go forth of *Sion*, and his Word from *Jerusalem*. Be not backward in discharging that great Trust committed to you in your respective Offices and Places, that you may be help-meets in the Restroration.

And be careful to suppress, and keep down all Vice, and disorderly Spirits, and incourage Virtue, not only in the general, but every one in his perticular Family; there is an incumbant Duty lieth on all Masters of Families over their Family, therefore my desire is, that we may call our Families together at convenient times and Seasons, to wait upon the Lord, and to seek to him for *Wisdom* and *Counsel*, that his Blessings may attend us and our Families, and our Children may sit about our Table as Olive-branches full of Virtue, then shall we be full of Joy and Peace, and living Praises will spring to the Lord, in that his Blessings and Fatherly Care hath been thus continued towards us.

Dear Friends; be tender and helpful one towards another, that the Lord may bless and fill you with his divine Love,

and

and fweet refrefhing Life, which unities our Souls to each other, and makes us as one Family of Love together : Let us not entertain any hard Thoughts one of another, but if difference fhould happen amongft us, let a fpeedy and peace-able end be put unto it ; for if Prejudices enter, it will eat out the precious Life, and make us barren and unfruitful to God. We are not without our daily Exercifes, Tryals and Temptations, therefore do defire the Lord may put it into your Hearts, to Pray for our Prefervation, and our fafe re-turn to you, that we may meet together again in the fame overcoming Love of God, in which we parted from you.

My Heart is full of Love to you, and do long to fee your Faces, and to enjoy your Company, that I may more fully exprefs that pure Love of God that fprings in my Heart unto you, then I can do by Writing. Therefore I defire you may reft fatisfied with thefe few Lines, and receive them as a token of unfeigned Love. From

Your dear Friend,

London, the 29th ⎞
  of the 8th ⎬
  Month, 1684. ⎠

Thomas Budd.

Some

Some material Things omitted in the foregoing part.

IT is to be noted, that the Tide runs to the Falls of *Delavvare*, it being one hundred and fifty Miles from the Capes, or entrance of the said River (which Falls, is a ledge of Rocks lying a cross the River) and also it runs up in some of the Cricks, ten or fifteen Miles, the said River and Cricks being navigable for Ships of great Burthen, there having lain over against *Burlington*, a Ship of about the burthen of four hundred Tuns afloat in four Fathom, at dead low Water, and the Flood riseth six or eight Foot; and there being no Worm that eats the bottoms of the Ships, as is usually done in *Virginia* and *Barbadoes*, &c. which renders the said Countries very fit for Trade and Navigation : And in the said River and Cricks are many other sorts of good *Fish*, not already named, some of which are *Cat-fish*, *Trout*, *Eales*, *Pearch*, &c.

ERRATA.

Page 13. line 16 after *often*, read *as*.   Page 25 l. 3 for *seven*, r. two hundred. line 19. f. 60 r. 6, l. 31 after *Beans*, r. *at three Shillings*.   Pag. 26 l 14 f. *I intend*, r. *I indent*. l. 22 f. *intend*, r. *indent*. pag. 28 l. 11 dele *and*.   Pag. 17 f. *ths*, r. *this*. l. 21 after *in*, r. *the*.